simply shetland 5
Roxana's Garden

For Simply Shetland 5, we invite you to open the gate and step into Roxana's Garden. Located in Napa, California, the garden is a wonderful blend of spots filled with sunshine and shade, where the fragrance of roses mingles with the herbal scent of lavender. We found this setting of lush foliage and bright flowers an irresistible backdrop for the projects in this volume.

Wander down the flagstone paths and explore the various garden rooms Roxana has created from reclaimed materials and growing plants. You don't know what you might find: an old wooden swing to curl up in, or the perfect spot for a tea party, or yet another gate under an archway of roses that beckons you to open it.

Just as Roxana's garden is awash in color, there are projects here that are sure to please the knitter who loves color—from the deeply intense colors and drapey drama of the *Annalisa Cape*, to the bright colorplay of the *Whirligig Vest*, to the rich mixing of two related colors in the *Clematis Jacket*. Just as Roxana's garden makes the most of climbing flowers and low creepers and everything in-between, these three projects ask you to flex your knitting skills: from mosaic knitting, to Fair Isle, to using crocheted embellishment to enhance "plain" knitting.

At the center of Roxana's garden is an arbor dedicated to white flowers that reminds us that neutrals have a soothing power all their own; sometimes we knitters long for the quiet sophistication of a single, subtle color. The *Roxana Jacket* is one of those projects that knitters dream of, because it looks more complicated to knit than it really is, and the final product will look good on many different body types; the *Greystone Vest* mimics the solid texture of stone in a chic, dress-it-up-or-dress-it-down way; the *Chevron Tunic* is a testament to the power and grace of a neutral color.

This volume includes two handsome sweaters for men, both easy to knit. We wander out of the garden briefly to showcase the *French Twist Pullover* in a setting of music and literature—what would a garden be without these?

The garden is a place where we can cast off the busy pace of our work world and, instead, enjoy a leisurely moment in the natural world. And knitting promises much the same: a leisurely moment to cast on and enjoy the natural fibers that are Jamieson's and Simply Shetland yarns.

May your knitting flower this season!

CONTENTS

UNICORN
BOOKS AND CRAFTS, INC.

vines tunic

tammy thompson

MATERIALS

YARN: Jamieson's Shetland Lambswool & Cashmere - 550 (600, 650, 700) grams. Shown in Eros (038).
NEEDLES: 16 & 32" circular and set of double-pointed US 6 (4 mm), *or correct needles to obtain gauge*.
ACCESSORIES: Stitch markers. Stitch holders.

MEASUREMENTS

CHEST: 35 (39, 40½, 42½)".
LENGTH TO ARMHOLE: 20".
ARMHOLE DEPTH: 9".
LENGTH: 29".
SLEEVE LENGTH (CUFF TO UNDERARM): 18".

GAUGE

On US 6 in st st: 26 sts and 24 rows = 4".

BODY

With 32" US 6, CO 210 (225, 240, 255) sts. Join and place marker for beg of rnd. Knit 1 rnd. Purl 3 rnds. Knit 1 rnd. Work the 26 rnds of **Chart A**. Work 2 rnds in st st, inc'g 18 (27, 24, 21) sts evenly spaced on second rnd (228 (252, 264, 276) sts on needle). Begin **Chart B** and place marker after 114 (126, 132, 138) sts. Continue pattern as set until piece measures 20" from CO edge, ending after working Row 6 of **Chart B**. Set aside.

SLEEVES

With double-pointed US 6, CO 48 sts. Join and place marker for beg of rnd. Knit 1 rnd, Purl 3 rnds. Knit 1 rnd. Work the 26 rnds of **Chart C**. Knit 1 rnd. Purl 3 rnds. Work 2 rnds in st st, inc'g 13 (13, 19, 19) sts evenly on the 2nd rnd (61 (61, 67, 67) sts on needle). Rep the 6 rows of **Chart B**, marking the last st as the center underarm st, **AND AT SAME TIME**, inc 1 st before and after this center underarm st every 4th rnd 15 times (91 (91, 97, 97) sts on needle). *Change to 16" circular if desired when sts will fit comfortably on needle.* Work without further shaping until piece measures 18" from CO edge, ending after working Rnd 5 of **Chart B**. On the next rnd (Rnd 6 of **Chart B**), work to within 6 sts of marker, then place next 13 sts onto holder (78 (78, 84, 84) sts rem for sleeve).

ATTACH SLEEVES TO BODY

Working again with body, work to within 6 sts of marker, place next 13 sts onto holder. Join sleeves to body as follows: place marker; work 78 (78, 84, 84) sts of one sleeve onto body needle; place marker work across body to within 6 sts of next marker; place next 13 sts onto holder; place marker, work 78 (78, 84, 84) sts of second sleeve; place marker. *The sts on holders will be grafted together during finishing.*

Continue in pattern as set, **AND AT SAME TIME**, dec every other rnd as follows: work to within 3 sts of marker; *ssk, k1, slip marker, k2tog; work to within 2 sts of next marker; k2tog, slip marker, k1, ssk**; work across back to within 3 sts of 3rd marker and rep from * to **. Continue to dec as described above until 30 (30, 36, 36) sts rem for sleeves and 53 (65, 71, 77) sts rem for front and for back, ending after working an even-numbered row of pattern (166 (190, 214, 226) sts on needle).

At beg of next rnd, break yarn. Slip next 17 (21, 23, 25) sts to right-hand needle and place next 19 (23, 25, 27) sts onto holder (these are center front neck sts). Rejoin yarn to work at right neck edge and continue in pattern as set (147 (167, 189, 199) sts on needle). *From this point on, work back and forth in rows, reading odd-numbered rows (RS) of Chart B*

from right to left and even-numbered rows (WS) from left to right. **AT SAME TIME**, dec at both neck edges every other row 5 times, working dec's on RS of garment as follows: *k1, ssk, knit to within 3 sts of end of rnd; k2tog, k1.* Work without further shaping on rem 137 (157, 179, 189) sts until garment measures 29" from CO edge, ending with RS facing for next row.

NECKBAND

With 16" circular US 6, beg at right neck edge, knit back neck sts, pick up 5 sts down left neck edge, knit 19 (23, 25, 27) front neck sts, pick up 5 sts up right neck edge (166, 190, 214, 226) sts on needle). Join and place marker for beg of rnd. Knit 2 rnds, dec'g evenly to 96 (96, 108, 120) sts on 2nd rnd. Work Rnds 1-16 of **Chart C**. Knit 1 rnd. Purl 2 rnds. BO loosely.

FINISHING

Weave in ends. Graft underarms from sts on holders. Block gently to finished measurements.

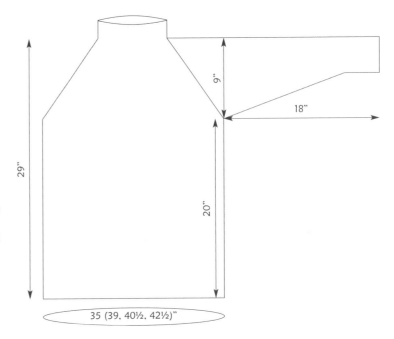

29"

20"

9"

18"

35 (39, 40½, 42½)"

Chart A

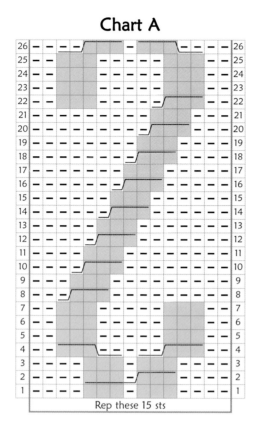

Rep these 15 sts

Chart B

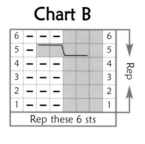

Rep these 6 sts

Rep

Chart C

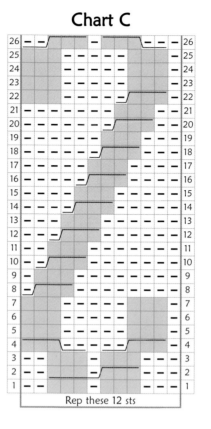

Rep these 12 sts

Key

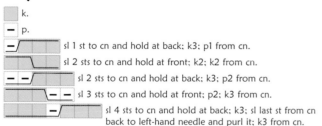

k.

— p.

— ⟋ sl 1 st to cn and hold at back; k3; p1 from cn.

sl 2 sts to cn and hold at front; k2; k2 from cn.

— — ⟋ sl 2 sts to cn and hold at back; k3; p2 from cn.

⟍ — — sl 3 sts to cn and hold at front; p2; k3 from cn.

— ⟋ sl 4 sts to cn and hold at back; k3; sl last st from cn
back to left-hand needle and purl it; k3 from cn.

slip stitch pullover

beatrice smith

MATERIALS

YARN: Simply Shetland Lambswool & Cashmere - 600 (700, 750, 850) grams. Shown in Vista (168).
NEEDLES: US 4 (3.5 mm) and US 6 (4 mm), *or correct needles to obtain gauge*. 16" circular US 4.

MEASUREMENTS

CHEST: 39 (42, 45, 48, 51)".
LENGTH TO UNDERARM: 14 (14½, 15, 15½, 16)".
ARMHOLE DEPTH: 9 (9½, 10, 10½, 11)".
LENGTH: 23 (24, 25, 26, 27)".
SLEEVE LENGTH: 19 (20, 21, 22, 23)".

GAUGE

On US 6 in **Slip Stitch Pattern:** 22 sts and 45 rows = 4".

SLIP STITCH PATTERN (MULTIPLE OF 16 STS + 12)

Rows 1 & 3 (RS): K12; sl 1, k2, sl 1; k12.
Row 2 (WS): K12; sl1 wyif, k2, sl 1 wyif; k12.
Row 4: K12; p1, k2, p1; k12.

Rep Rows 1-4.

BACK

With 24" US 4, CO 94 (102, 110, 118, 122) sts and work ribbing as follows:

Row 1 (WS): ([K2, p2] 2 (3, 4, 5, 2) times), k2; *p1, k2, p1; ([k2, p2] 2 times), k2; rep from * 4 (4, 4, 4, 6) times; p1, k2, p1; ([k2, p2] 2 (3, 4, 5, 2) times), k2.
Row 2 (RS): ([P2, k2] 2 (3, 4, 5, 2) times), p2; *k4; ([p2, k2] 2 times), p2; rep from * 4 (4, 4, 4, 6) times; k4; ([p2, k2] 2 (3, 4, 5, 2) times), p2.

Rep Rows 1-2 until ribbing measures 2½" from CO edge, ending with WS facing for next row. Work incs for body as follows:

Next Row (WS) (Inc Row): Work 3 (3, 7, 7, 3) sts in ribbing as set, m1p, k4 (8, 4, 8, 4) sts in ribbing as set, m1p, work 3 (3, 7, 7, 3) sts in ribbing as set; *p1, k2, p1; work 3 sts in ribbing as set, m1p, work 4 sts in ribbing as set, m1p, work 3 sts in ribbing as set; rep from * 4 (4, 4, 4, 6) times; p1, k2, p1; work 3 (3, 7, 7, 3) sts in ribbing as set, m1p, work 4 (8,

4, 8, 4) sts in ribbing as set, m1p, work 3 (3, 7, 7, 3) sts in ribbing as set (108 (116, 124, 132, 140) sts on needle).

Change to US 6 and continue as follows:

Rows 1 & 3 (RS): K12 (16, 20, 24, 12); *sl 1, k2, sl 1; k12; rep from * 4 (4, 4, 4, 6) times; sl 1, k2, sl 1; k12 (16, 20, 24, 12).
Row 2 (WS): k12 (16, 20, 24, 12); *sl 1 wyif, k2, sl 1 wyif; k12; rep from * 4 (4, 4, 4, 6) times; sl 1 wyif, k2, sl 1 wyif; k12 (16, 20, 24, 12).
Row 4 (WS): K12 (16, 20, 24, 12); *p1, k2, p1; k12; rep from * 4 (4, 4, 4, 6) times; p1, k2, p1; k12 (16, 20, 24, 12).

Rep Rows 1-4 until piece measures 14 (14½, 15, 15½, 16)" from CO edge, ending with RS facing for next row.

SHAPE UNDERARMS

Continuing in pattern as set, BO 5 sts at beg of next 2 rows, then dec 1 st at beg and end of next 5 rows. Continue as set on rem 88 (96, 104, 112, 120) sts until piece measures 23 (24, 25, 26, 27)" from CO edge, ending after working Row 3 of stitch pattern and with WS facing for next row.

Next Row (WS) (Row 4 of Stitch Pattern): Work first 22 (26, 30, 34, 38) sts and place on holder for right shoulder, work next 44 sts and place on holder for back neck, work rem 22 (26, 30, 34, 38) sts and place on holder for left shoulder.

FRONT

Work same as for back until piece measures 20 (21, 22, 23, 24)" from CO edge, ending after working row 3 of stitch pattern and with WS facing for next row.

SHAPE FRONT NECK

Next Row (WS) (Row 4 of Stitch Pattern): Work 34 (38, 42, 46, 50) sts, work next 20 sts and place on holder for front neck, work rem 34 (38, 42, 56, 50) sts.

Turn, and working each side separately, dec 1 st at neck edge on every RS row 12 times. Work without further shaping on rem 22 (26, 30, 34, 38) sts until front measures same as back. Place shoulder sts on holders.

JOIN SHOULDERS

With RS's facing, join shoulders using 3-needle bind-off method.

SLEEVES

With US 4, CO 50 sts and work ribbing as follows:

Row 1 (WS): K2; *p1, k2, p1; ([k2, p2] 2 times), k2; rep from * 2 times; p1, k2, p1; k2.
Row 2 (RS): P2; *k4; ([p2, k2] 2 times), p2; rep from * 2 times; k4; p2.

Rep Rows 1-2 until ribbing measures 2" from CO edge, ending with WS facing for next row. Work incs for body as follows:

Next Row (WS) (Inc Row): K2; *p1, k2, p1; work 3 sts in ribbing as set, m1p, work 4 sts in ribbing as set, m1p, work 3 sts in ribbing as set; rep from * 2 times; p1, k2, p1; k2 (56 sts on needle).

Change to US 6 and continue as follows:

Rows 1 & 3 (RS): K2; *sl 1, k2, sl 1; k12; rep from 2 times; sl 1, k2, sl 1; k2.
Row 2 (WS): K2; *sl 1 wyif, k2, sl 1 wyif; k12; rep from * 2 times; sl 1 wyif, k2, sl 1 wyif; k2.
Row 4 (WS): K2; *p1, k2, p1; k12; rep from * 2 times; p1, k2, p1; k2.

Rep Rows 1-4, **AND AT SAME TIME**, inc 1 st at beg and end of every 6th row 0 (6, 12, 18, 21) times, every 8th row 20 (18, 15, 12, 11) times, and every 10th row 1 (0, 0, 0, 0) times (98 (104, 110, 116, 120) sts on needle). Work without further shaping until sleeve measures 18¼ (19¼, 20¼, 21¼, 22¼)" from CO edge, ending with RS facing for next row. BO 5 sts at beg of next 2 rows, then dec 1 st at beg and end of next 5 rows. BO rem 78 (84, 90, 96, 100) sts.

NECKBAND

With 16" US 4, RS facing, work sts from back neck holder as follows: *p2, k1, k2tog, p2, k2tog, k1, p2, k4; rep from * once; p2, k1, k2tog, p2, k2tog, k1, p2; pick up 20 sts down left neck edge; work sts from front neck holder as follows: k4, p2, k1, k2tog, p2, k2tog, k1, p2, k4; pick up 20 sts up right neck edge (96 sts on needle). Join and work in the rnd as follows:

Rnd 1: *([P2, k2] twice), p2; k1, p2, k1; rep from * once; ([p2, k2] twice), p2; ([k2, p2] 5 times); k1, p2, k1; ([p2, k2] twice), p2; k1, p2, k1; ([p2, k2] 5 times).
Rnd 2: *([p2, k2] twice), p2; k4; rep from * once; ([p2, k2] twice), p2; ([k2, p2] 5 times); k4; ([p2, k2] twice, p2; k4; ([p2, k2] 5 times).

Rep Rnds 1-2 until neckband measures 1¼". BO loosely.

FINISHING

Sew sleeves into armholes. Sew side and sleeve seams. Weave in ends. Block gently.

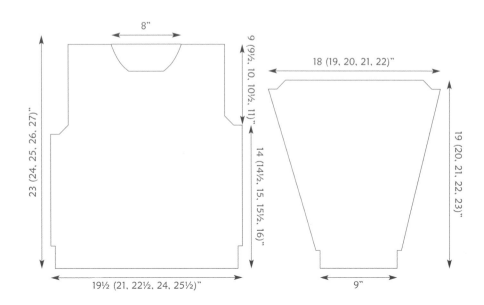

french barrel wrap

beatrice smith

MATERIALS
YARN: Simply Shetland Lambswool & Cashmere - 500 grams.
Shown in Snow (200).
NEEDLES: US 9 (5.5 mm), *or correct needles to obtain gauge.*

MEASUREMENTS
WIDTH: 14".
LENGTH (NOT INCLUDING TASSELS): 68".

GAUGE
On US 9 in **Stitch Pattern**: 31 sts and 32 rows = 4"
after blocking.

STITCH PATTERN (MULTIPLE OF 10 STS + 8)
Rows 1, 3 & 5 (WS): K1; *k6, p4; rep from *; end k7.
Rows 2 & 6 (RS): K1; *p6, sl next 2 sts to cn and hold at back, k2, k2 from cn; rep from *; end p6, k1.
Row 4: K1; *p6, yo, k2tog tbl, k2tog, yo; rep from *; end p6, k1.
Row 7: K1; *k3tog tbl, k3tog, pass the first of these 2 sts over the second, p4; rep from * to last 7 sts; k3tog tbl, k3tog, pass the first of these 2 sts over the second, k1.
Row 8: K1; *([k1, p1] 3 times in the next st, making 6 sts from 1 st), yo, k2tog tbl, k2tog, yo; rep from *; end ([k1, p1] 3 times in next st, making 6 sts from 1 st), k1.

Rep Rows 1-8.

WRAP
CO 108 sts. Work in **Stitch Pattern** until piece measures 68".
BO.

FINISHING
Weave in ends. Block gently. If desired, make tassels and attach to short ends.

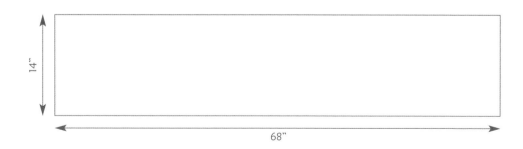

14"

68"

clematis jacket

carol lapin

MATERIALS

YARN: Simply Shetland Lambswool & Cashmere - 650 (700) grams MC and 150 grams CC. Garment shown in MC Red Hot (1294) and CC Petunia (344).
NEEDLES: US 4 (3.5 mm) and US 6 (4 mm), *or correct needles to obtain gauge.*
ACCESSORIES: Stitch holders.

MEASUREMENTS
WIDTH: 39½ (44)".
LENGTH: 18".
SLEEVE LENGTH: 7½".

GAUGE
On US 6 in **Stitch Pattern**: 22 sts and 28 rows = 4".

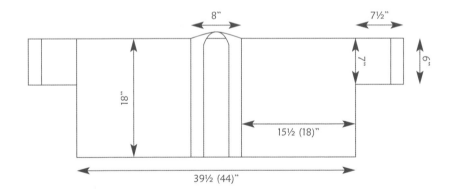

STITCH PATTERN (MULTIPLE OF 12 STS + 2 EDGE STS)
Row 1 (RS): Edge st, k5; *p2, k10; rep from * to last 8 sts; end p2, k5, edge st.
Row 2: Edge st, p4; *k1, p2, k1, p8; rep from * to last 9 sts; end k1, p2, k1, p4, edge st.
Row 3: Edge st, k3; *p1, k4, p1, k6; rep from * to last 10 sts; end p1, k4, p1, k3, edge st.
Row 4: Edge st, p2; *k1, p6, k1, p4; rep from * to last 11 sts; end k1, p6, k1, p2, edge st.
Row 5: Edge st, k1; *p1, k8, p1, k2; rep from * to last 12 sts; end p1, k8, p1, k1, edge st.
Row 6: Edge st, k1; *p10, k2; rep from * to last 12 sts; p10, k1, edge st.
Row 7, 9, 11 & 13: Knit.
Row 8, 10, 12 & 14: Purl.

Rep Rows 1-14.

BACK
With US 4 and MC, CO 218 (242) sts.

Next Row: *K1, p1; rep from *.

Rep this row until ribbing measures 1" from CO edge, ending with RS facing for next row. Change to US 6 and work 4 rows in st st. Rep the 14 rows of **Stitch Pattern** until piece measures 18", ending after working Row 10 of **Stitch Pattern**.

Next Row (RS): Work 86 (98) sts, BO next 46 sts for back neck, work rem 86 (98) sts.

Place shoulder sts on holders.

LEFT FRONT
With US 4 and MC, CO 86 (98) sts. Work same as for back until piece measures 18", ending after working Row 10 of **Stitch Pattern**. Place sts on holder.

RIGHT FRONT
Work same as for left front.

JOIN SHOULDERS
Join shoulders using 3-needle bind-off method.

SLEEVES
Place markers 7" down from shoulder seam on both front and back along armhole edge. With US 6 and MC, RS facing, pick up 86 sts evenly between markers. Work in st st for 3 rows. Rep the 14 rows of **Stitch Pattern** twice, then work through Row 8. BO.

FRONT BAND
With US 4 and MC, CO 34 sts.

Rows 1 & 3 (RS): With MC, knit.
Rows 2 & 4: With MC, purl.
Row 5: With CC, knit.
Row 6: With CC, p17, k17.

Rep Rows 1-6 until piece measures approx. 43½", then work Rows 1-4. BO. *Band should fit comfortably along front edges of jacket and back neck; make band shorter or longer if necessary.* Sew band to jacket, fold in half and stitch to inside.

SLEEVE CUFFS
Work same as for front band until piece measures approx. 12". BO. Sew cuff to sleeve, easing in extra sleeve fabric. Fold band in half and stitch to inside.

FINISHING
Sew side and sleeve seams. Weave in ends. Block gently.

SURFACE DECORATION
With CC and #2 or #3 crochet hook, RS facing, work slip st crochet in each purl bump across jacket following zig zag pattern. Work in same manner for sleeves. Weave in ends.

rose tunic

carol lapin

MATERIALS

YARN: Simply Shetland Lambswool & Cashmere - 350 (350, 400, 450) grams. Shown in Petunia (344).
Optional—10 yards Red Hot (1294) for crochet edge around armholes and neck.
NEEDLES: US 5 (3.75 mm) and US 6 (4 mm), *or correct needles to obtain gauge.*

MEASUREMENTS

AT BOTTOM: 43 (46½, 50, 53)".
CHEST: 36 (39, 42½, 46)".
LENGTH (INCLUDING POINTS): 23½ (24, 24½, 25)".

GAUGE

On US 6 in garter st: 22 sts and 40 rows = 4".

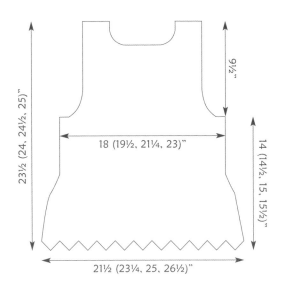

9½"

23½ (24, 24½, 25)"

18 (19½, 21¼, 23)"

14 (14½, 15, 15½)"

21½ (23¼, 25, 26½)"

SPECIAL ABBREVIATIONS

W&T (wrap & turn)—With yarn in back, sl next st as if to purl. Bring yarn to front of work and sl st back to left-hand needle. Turn work.

BACK

MAKE POINTED BORDER
*With US 5, CO 2 sts.

Row 1: Knit.
Rows 2-11 (12, 13, 14): Knit into front and back of first st; knit to end.

After Row 11 (12, 13, 14), there are 13 (14, 15, 16) sts on needle. Break yarn and leave point on needle. Rep from * until there are 9 points on needle.

Next Row (RS): Knit across all points, **AND AT SAME TIME**, inc 1 st at beg and end of row (119 (128, 137, 146) sts on needle and all 9 points are joined).

Change to US 6 and continue in garter st without shaping until piece measures 3 (3½, 4, 4½)" (not including points). Continue in garter st, **AND AT SAME TIME**, dec 1 st at beg and end of every 6th row 10 times (99 (108, 117, 126) sts on needle). Work without shaping until piece measures 14 (14½, 15, 15½)" (not including points), ending with RS facing for next row.

SHAPE ARMHOLES
BO 6 sts at beg of next 2 rows.

Next Row (RS) (Dec Row): K3, ssk; work to last 5 sts; k2tog, k3.

Continue in garter st, working **Dec Row** every other row 12 more times. Continue without further shaping on rem 61 (70, 79, 88) sts until piece measures 21½ (22, 22½, 23)" (not including points), ending with RS facing for next row.

SHAPE BACK NECK
Next Row (RS): K15 (17, 19, 21); BO next 31 (36, 41, 46) sts for back neck; k15 (17, 19, 21).

Turn and work left side only as follows:

Next Row (WS): Knit.
Next Row (RS): BO 2 sts (13 (15, 17, 19) sts rem).
Next Row (WS): Knit.

SHAPE SHOULDER
Next Row (RS): K8 (10, 12, 14), W&T.
Next Row (WS): Knit.
Next Row (RS): K4 (5, 6, 7), W&T.
Next Row (WS): Knit.

Break yarn, leaving 12" tail and place left shoulder sts on holder. Reattach yarn and work right side same as for left side, reversing shaping. Place right shoulder sts on holder.

FRONT

Work same as for back until piece measures 18½ (19, 19½, 20)" (not including points), ending with RS facing for next row.

SHAPE FRONT NECK
Next Row (RS): K26 (30, 33, 36); BO next 9 (10, 13, 16) sts for front neck; k26 (30, 33, 36).

Turn and working left side only, BO 3 (3, 3, 3) sts twice, 2 sts 2 (3, 3, 3) times and 1 st 3 (3, 4, 5) times (13 (15, 17, 19) sts rem). Work without shaping until you are 4 rows short of back, then shape shoulder same as for back. Break yarn, leaving 12" tail and place left shoulder sts on holder. Reattach yarn and work right side same as for left side, reversing shaping. Place right shoulder sts on holder.

JOIN SHOULDERS
With WS's facing each other and RS's facing you, join shoulders using 3-needle bind-off method. This makes a garter ridge on RS of garment.

FINISHING
Sew side seams. If desired, work slip st crochet around armhole and neck edges with either Red Hot or Petunia.

farmers' market vest

 doreen marquart

MATERIALS

YARN: Simply Shetland Lambswool & Cashmere - 200 (200, 250, 250, 300, 300) grams of MC; 100 (100, 150, 150, 200, 200) grams of CC 1; 100 (100, 150, 150, 200, 200) grams of CC 2. Shown in MC Sienna (156), CC 1 Cumin (262), and CC 2 Olive Grove (1057).
NEEDLES: 24" circular US 5 (3.75 mm), *or correct needles to obtain gauge.* Size E crochet hook.
ACCESSORIES: Stitch holders. "Locking pin" stitch markers. 5 (5, 5, 6, 6, 6) ¾" buttons.

MEASUREMENTS

CHEST: 34 (38, 42, 46, 50, 54)".
LENGTH TO UNDERARM: 10½ (11, 11, 12, 13, 13)".
ARMHOLE DEPTH: 9 (9, 10, 10, 11, 12)".
LENGTH (NOT INCLUDING CROCHET EDGE; THIS WILL ADD APPROX. ½"): 19½ (20, 21, 22, 24, 25)".

GAUGE

On US 5 in garter st: 22 sts and 40 rows = 4".

DESIGNER NOTES

Knitted entirely in garter stitch, this vest is completely reversible. It not only buttons down the front; it also buttons down the back. Wear it frontwards, backwards, or inside out. See schematic.

STRIPE PATTERN

Use MC throughout and CC 1 or CC 2 as specified.

Rows 1-2: With MC, knit—1 ridge. *Mark Row 1 as RS.*
Rows 3-6: With CC, knit—2 ridges.
Rows 7-12: With MC, knit—3 ridges.
Rows 13-14: With CC knit—1 ridge.
Rows 15-18: With MC, knit—2 ridges.
Rows 19-24: With CC, knit—3 ridges.

Rep Rows 1-24.

Don't cut yarns when changing colors. Carry them neatly along edge. You'll add a crocheted trim over edges during finishing.

PIECE A (WORKED FROM BOTTOM TO TOP)

With MC, CO 50 (55, 60, 66, 72, 78) sts.

With MC and CC 1, work 104 (110, 110, 120, 130, 130) rows in **Stripe Pattern**, ending with RS facing for next row.

SHAPE ARMHOLE

BO 9 (12, 12, 16, 18, 22) sts at beg of next row. Continue in pattern as set on rem 41 (43, 48, 50, 54, 56) sts until there are 161 (167, 171, 181, 197, 207) rows from CO edge, ending with WS facing for next row.

SHAPE NECK

BO 18 (18, 20, 22, 22, 24) sts at beg of next row. Continue in pattern as set on rem 23 (25, 28, 28, 32, 32) sts until there are 194 (200, 210, 220, 240, 250) rows from CO edge, ending after working a WS row. Break yarns and place shoulder sts on holder.

With E crochet hook and MC, RS facing, work 57 (60, 60, 66, 72, 72) single crochet sts along "side seam" edge, beg at bottom and working up towards underarm. Break yarn.

PIECE B (PICKED UP ALONG "SIDE SEAM" EDGE OF PIECE A)

With MC, RS facing, beg at lower edge, pick up 57 (60, 60, 66, 72, 72) sts through both loops of single crochet sts along "side seam" edge of Piece A. *This is Row 1 of **Stripe Pattern**.*

With MC and CC 2, beg with Row 2, work 15 (21, 21, 29, 31, 39) rows in **Stripe Pattern**. CO 50 (52, 55, 56, 60, 66) sts at end of last (RS) row as follows: Turn. *Insert right-hand needle between 1st and 2nd sts on left-hand needle, wrap yarn around right-needle and pull loop through, twist, and place on left-hand needle; rep from * (107 (112, 115, 122, 132, 138) sts on needle).

CONTINUE PIECE B AND JOIN TO PIECE A AT SHOULDERS
With WS facing, beg at neck edge, slide the 23 (25, 28, 28, 32, 32) shoulder sts of Piece A from holder onto left-hand needle. Leaving these sts unknitted, work across the sts you just cast on and those you have been working on. Continue pattern as set, **AND AT SAME TIME**, on every RS row, knit the last stitch tog with the next Piece A shoulder stitch. Continue in this manner until all the shoulder sts are joined, ending with WS facing for next row.

SHAPE NECK
BO 19 (19, 22, 22, 24, 24) at beg of next row, work to end of row. Continue pattern as set on rem 88 (93, 93, 100, 108, 114) sts until there are 90 (100, 108, 120, 132, 144) rows in Piece B, ending after working a WS row. BO.

MARK FOR BUTTON/BUTTONHOLE PLACEMENT
On Piece A, mark 3rd (3rd, 4th, 4th, 4th, 3rd) garter ridge from bottom edge for button/buttonhole placement. Continue placing markers with 18 (19, 19, 20, 22, 24) ridges between each marked ridge. This should leave 2 (1, 2, 3, 3, 1) ridge(s) at top (neck) edge.

On Piece B, mark button/buttonhole placement beg on row 85 (95, 103, 115, 127, 139) (3rd ridge from finished edge—beg on RS of piece).

PIECE C
With MC and CC 2, work same as for Piece A, **AND AT SAME TIME**, work **Buttonhole Rows** (described below) on rows that correspond to those marked on Piece B.

BUTTONHOLE ROWS
Row 1 (RS): Work to last 4 sts, BO 2, k2.
Row 2: K2, CO 2, work to end of row.

PIECE D
With MC and CC1, work same as for Piece B, **AND AT SAME TIME**, work **Buttonhole Rows** (described below) on rows that correspond to those marked on Piece A.

BUTTONHOLE ROWS
Row 1 (RS): K1 (1, 1, 1, 3, 3), BO 2; *k19 (20, 20, 17, 18, 19), BO 2; rep from * 3 (3, 3, 4, 4, 4) more times; end k1 (2, 2, 2, 3, 4).
Row 2: K1 (2, 2, 2, 3, 4); CO 2, *k19 (20, 20, 17, 18, 19), CO 2; rep from * 3 (3, 3, 4, 4, 4) more times; end k1 (1, 1, 1, 3, 3).

Work 4 rows. BO on RS.

FINISHING
Work crochet edge around outside edge of each piece as follows:

Rnd 1: Beg at lower side seam, work single crochet evenly around entire outside edge of vest, placing 2-3 single crochet sts in corners to lay them flat. Join with slip stitch to first single crochet. Don't break yarn.

Rnd 2: Chain 1, do not turn work, and work backwards single crochet around entire edge.

Work as above around armholes, beg at underarm seam. Weave in ends. Sew on buttons opposite buttonholes. Block gently.

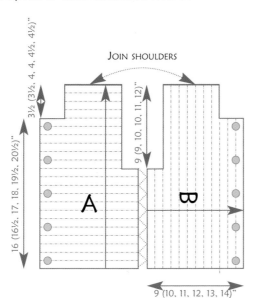

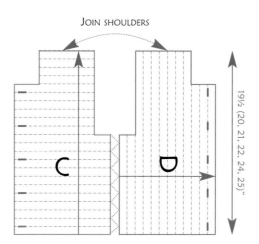

3-button wrap

prudence makepeace

MATERIALS

YARN: Simply Shetland Lambswool & Cashmere - 400 grams. Hold 2 strands together throughout. Shown in Mallard (555).
NEEDLES: 24" US 10 (6 mm), **or correct needles to obtain gauge.**
ACCESSORIES: Three 2" buttons.

MEASUREMENTS
WIDTH: 16".
LENGTH: 60".

GAUGE
On US 10 in st st: 14 sts and 20 rows = 4".

WRAP
CO 56 sts.

Row 1 (RS): Sl 1 pwise, knit to end of row.
Row 2 (WS): Sl 1 pwise, purl to end of row.

Rep these 2 rows until piece measures 9½" from CO edge, ending with RS facing for next row.

MAKE BUTTONHOLE
Next Row (RS): K13; pass yarn between needles to front, sl 1 st from left-hand needle to right-hand needle, pass yarn between needles to back and leave hanging; *sl 1 st from left-hand needle to right-hand needle, pass the 1st st over it; rep from * 7 times; sl the last bound-off st back to left-hand needle and turn work; pass yarn previously hanging between needles to back; **insert right-hand needle between 1st and 2nd sts on left-hand needle, wrap yarn around right-hand needle and pull loop through, twist, and place on left-hand needle; rep from ** 8 times *(you'll have one more cast-on st than you bound off)*. Before placing last loop on left-hand needle, pass yarn between needles to front; turn; sl the first st from left-hand needle to right-hand needle; pass the last st over it. Knit to end of row.

Continue in pattern as set until piece measures 60" from CO edge. BO.

FINISHING
Weave in ends. Block gently. Sew buttons to align with buttonhole 9", 13½" and 18" from other end of wrap opposite buttonhole (see schematic).

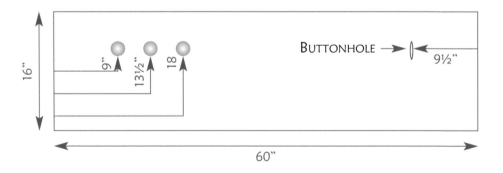

greystone vest

doreen marquart

MATERIALS

YARN: Simply Shetland Lambswool & Cashmere - 200 (250, 300, 350) grams. Shown in Flannel (030).
NEEDLES: US 5 (3.75 mm), *or correct needles to obtain gauge.*
ACCESSORIES: Stitch holders. Stitch markers. Six ¾" buttons.

MEASUREMENTS

CHEST: 34 (39, 45, 51)".
LENGTH TO UNDERARM: 9 (10, 10, 11)".
ARMHOLE DEPTH: 9 (9, 10, 10)".
LENGTH: 18 (19, 20, 21)".

GAUGE

On US 5 in garter st: 22 sts and 40 rows = 4".

DESIGNER NOTE

Because of the different natures of the stitches used in adjoining panels (double moss, ribbing and garter stitches), it is especially necessary to block this vest. For the most accurate vertical measurement, measure over the double moss panel (indicated by an asterisk (*) on the schematic.

BACK

CO 92 (106, 122, 140) sts.

Row 1 (RS): ([K2, p2] 3 (3, 4, 5) times); pm; k1; pm; ([p2, k2] 5 (6, 7, 8) times); pm; k1; pm; k24 (30, 30, 32); pm; k1; pm; ([k2, p2] 5 (6, 7, 8) times); pm; k1; pm; ([p2, k2] 3 (3, 4, 5) times).

Row 2: ([P2, k2] 3 (3, 4, 5) times); sl 1 wyif; ([k2, p2] 5 (6, 7, 8) times); sl 1 wyif; k24 (30, 30, 32); sl 1 wyif; ([p2, k2] 5 (6, 7, 8) times); sl 1 wyif; ([k2, p2] 3 (3, 4, 5) times).

Row 3: ([K2, p2] 3 (3, 4, 5) times); k1; ([k2, p2] 5 (6, 7, 8) times); k1; k24 (30, 30, 32); k1; ([p2, k2] 5 (6, 7, 8) times); k1; ([p2, k2] 3 (3, 4, 5) times).

Row 4: ([P2, k2] 3 (3, 4, 5) times); sl 1 wyif; ([p2, k2] 5 (6, 7, 8) times; sl 1 wyif; k24 (30, 30, 32); sl 1 wyif; ([k2, p2] 5 (6, 7, 8) times); sl 1 wyif; ([k2, p2] 3 (3, 4, 5) times).

Rep these 4 rows until back measures 9 (10, 10, 11)" from CO edge, ending after working Row 4 of pattern.

SHAPE UNDERARMS

Continuing as set, BO 12 (12, 16, 20) sts at beg of next 2 rows. Work without shaping on rem 68 (82, 90, 100) sts until back measures 14 (14, 15, 15)" from CO edge, ending after working Row 4 of pattern.

SHAPE BACK NECK

Next Row (RS): Work 34 (41, 45, 50) sts. Turn and work 1 WS row. Continuing in pattern as set, dec 1 st at neck edge on every RS row 12 (15, 15, 16) times. Continue on rem 22 (26, 30, 34) sts until armhole measures 9 (9, 10, 10)" ending after working Row 4 of stitch pattern. Place shoulder sts on holder. Rejoin yarn and work left neck same as for right.

LEFT FRONT

CO 35 (39, 47, 55) sts.

Row 1 (RS): ([K2, p2] 3 (3, 4, 5) times); pm; k1; pm; ([k2, p2] 5 (6, 7, 8) times); pm; k1; pm; k1.

Row 2: K1; sl 1 wyif; ([k2, p2] 5 (6, 7, 8) times); sl 1 wyif; ([k2, p2] 3 (3, 4, 5) times).

Row 3: ([K2, p2] 3 (3, 4, 5) times); k1; ([p2, k2] 5 (6, 7, 8) times); knit to end of row, inc'g in last st.

Row 4: Knit to first marker; sl 1 wyif; ([p2, k2] 5 (6, 7, 8) times); sl 1 wyif; ([k2, p2] 3 (3, 4, 5) times).

Rep these 4 rows, inc'g 1 st at end of every RS row 23 (29, 29, 31) times total, bringing these inc'd sts into garter stitch, ending with RS facing for next row (58 (68, 76, 86) sts on needle). Continue in pattern as set without shaping for 24 (26, 30, 34) more rows, ending with RS facing for next row.

Shape Left Front Neck and Underarm
Continuing in pattern as set, dec 1 st at end of every RS row 24 (30, 30, 32) times, **AND AT SAME TIME**, when work measures same as back to armhole, BO 12 (12, 16, 20) sts at beg of next RS row to shape underarm. Continue in pattern as set, still dec'g at end of every RS row, until 22 (26, 30, 34) sts rem. Work without further shaping until length measures same as back. Place shoulder sts on holder.

Right Front
CO 35 (39, 47, 55) sts.

Row 1 (RS): K1; pm; k1; pm; ([p2, k2] 5 (6, 7, 8) times); pm; k1; pm; ([p2, k2] 3 (3, 4, 5) times).

Row 2: ([P2, k2] 3 (3, 4, 5) times); sl 1 wyif; ([p2, k2] 5 (6, 7, 8) times); sl 1 wyif; k1.

Row 3: Inc in first st; knit to first marker; k1; ([k2, p2] 5 (6, 7, 8) times); k1; ([p2, k2] 3 (3, 4, 5) times).

Row 4: ([P2, k2] 3 (3, 4, 5) times); sl 1 wyif; ([k2, p2] 5 (6, 7, 8) times); sl 1 wyif; knit to end of row.

Rep these 4 rows, inc'g 1 st at beg of every RS row 23 (29, 29, 31) times total, bringing these inc'd sts into garter st, ending with RS facing for next row (58 (68, 76, 86) sts on needle). Continue in pattern as set without shaping for 2 (2, 4, 4) more rows.

Work Buttonhole Rows
Row 1 (RS): K3, BO 2 sts, k14 (20, 20, 22), BO 2 sts, work in pattern as set to end of row.

Row 2: Work in pattern as set, casting on 2 sts over each set of BO's from previous row.

Continue in pattern as set for 16 (18, 18, 22) more rows. Rep **Buttonhole Rows** once more. Continue without shaping for 2 (2, 4, 4) more rows. ending with RS facing for next row.

Shape Right Front Neck
Continuing in pattern as set, dec 1 st at beg of every RS row 24 (30, 30, 32) times, **AND AT SAME TIME**, when work measures same as back to armhole, BO 12 (12, 16, 20) sts at beg of next WS row to shape underarm. Continue in pattern as set, still dec'g at end of every RS row, until 22 (26, 30, 34) sts rem. Work without further shaping until length measures same as left front. Place shoulder sts on holder.

Join Shoulders
Join shoulders using 3-needle bind-off method.

Back Tab
CO 1 st.

Row 1 (RS): Inc in st (2 sts on needle).
Row 2: Knit.
Row 3: Inc in each st (4 sts on needle).
Row 4: Knit.
Row 5: Knit, inc'g in first and last st (6 sts on needle).
Row 6: Knit.

Rep Rows 5-6 until there are 8 (10, 12, 12) sts on needle. Work without shaping in garter st until tab measures 6 (7, 7, 8)" from CO edge, ending with RS facing for next row. Dec as follows:

Row 1 (RS): K2tog, knit to last 2 sts, k2 tog.
Row 2: Knit.

Rep Rows 1-2 until 2 sts rem, ending after working Row 2.

Next Row (RS): K2tog.

Break yarn. Pull tail through rem st and weave in end.

Finishing
Sew side seams. Sew on buttons opposite buttonholes. Sew back tab to back of vest so it lines up halfway between buttons on front (see schematic). Sew buttons to back tab points. Weave in ends. Block to finished measurements.

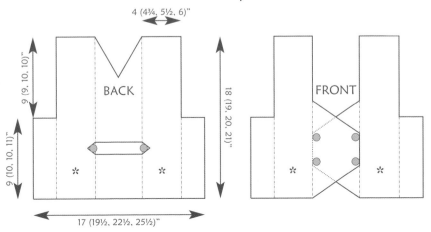

french twist pullover

beatrice smith

MATERIALS
YARN: In Simply Shetland Silk & Lambswool - 600 (650, 700, 750) grams. Hold 2 strands together throughout.
Shown in Glenbuchat (033).
NEEDLES: US 6 (4 mm) and US 7 (4.5 mm), *or correct needles to obtain gauge.*

MEASUREMENTS
CHEST: 36 (42, 48, 54)".
LENGTH TO UNDERARM: 14 (14, 14½, 15)".
ARMHOLE DEPTH: 9 (10, 10½, 11)".
LENGTH: 23 (24, 25, 26)".
SLEEVE LENGTH: 17 (18, 19, 21)".

GAUGE
On US 7 in **French Twist Pattern**: 22 sts and 28 rows = 4" (lightly stretched).

RIB PATTERN (MULTIPLE OF 7 STS + 3)
Rows 1 & 3 (WS): *K1, p1, k1, p4; rep from * to last 3 sts; k1, p1, k1.
Row 2: *P1, k1tbl, p1, k4; rep from * to last 3 sts; p1, k1tbl, p1.
Row 4: *P1, k1tbl, p1; sl 2 sts to cn and hold at back; k2; k2 from cn; rep from * to last 3 sts; p1, k1tbl, p1.

Rep Rows 1-4.

FRENCH TWIST PATTERN (MULTIPLE OF 8 STS + 4)
Row 1 (RS): *P4, yo, k2tog tbl, k2tog, yo; rep from * to last 4 sts; p4.
Rows 2 & 4: *K4, p4; rep from * to last 4 sts; k4.
Row 3: *P4, sl 2 sts to cn and hold at back, k2, k2 from cn; rep from * to last 4 sts; p4.

Rep Rows 1-4.

BACK
With US 6, CO 87 (101, 115, 129) sts. Work Rows 3-4 of **Rib Pattern** once, Rows 1-4 three times, and Rows 1-2 once.

Next Row (WS) (Inc Row): *K1, m1, k2, p4; rep from * to last 3 sts; k1, m1, k2 (100 (116, 132, 148) sts on needle).

Change to US 7 and work **French Twist Pattern** until piece measures 14 (14, 14½, 15)" from CO edge, ending with RS facing for next row.

SHAPE ARMHOLES
BO 4 sts at beg of next 2 rows, then dec 1 st and beg and end of every RS row 4 times. Work without further shaping on rem 84 (100, 116, 132) sts until armhole measures 9 (10, 10½, 11)", ending with RS facing for next row.

SHAPE BACK NECK
Next Row (RS): Work 24 (32, 40, 48) sts, place next 36 sts on holder for back neck. Turn and work WS row, dec'g 1 st at beg of row (neck edge). Place rem 23 (31, 39, 47) sts on holder for right shoulder. Break yarn, rejoin and work 24 (32, 40, 48) sts for left shoulder. Turn, and work WS row, dec'g 1 st at end of row (neck edge). Place rem 23 (31, 39, 47) sts on holder for left shoulder.

FRONT
Work same as for back until armhole measures 6 (7, 7½, 8)", ending with RS facing for next row.

SHAPE FRONT NECK
Next Row (RS): Work 32 (40, 48, 56) sts, place next 20 sts on holder for front neck. Turn, and working each side separately, dec 1 st at neck edge on every row 4 times, then

every other row 5 times. Work without further shaping on rem 23 (31, 39, 47) sts until front is same length as back.

JOIN SHOULDERS
Join shoulder using 3-needle bind-off method.

SLEEVES
With US 6, CO 52 sts. Work Rows 3-4 of **Rib Pattern** once, Rows 1-4 three times, and Rows 1-2 once.

Next Row (WS) (Inc Row): *K1, m1, k2, p4; rep from * to last 3 sts; k1, m1, k2 (60 sts on needle).

Change to US 7 and work **French Twist Pattern, AND AT SAME TIME,** inc 1 st at beg and end of every 4th row 10 (22, 26, 29) times, then every 6th row 8 (1, 0, 0) times, working inc'd sts into pattern (96, 106, 112, 118) sts on needle). Continue in pattern as set without further shaping until piece measures 16 (17, 18, 20)" from CO edge, ending with RS facing for next row.

SHAPE SLEEVE CAP
Dec 1 st at beg and end of every RS row 4 times. BO rem 88 (98, 104, 110) sts.

NECKBAND
With US 6, RS facing, ([p4, k4] 4 times), p4 from from back neck holder; pick up 1 st between back neck and left shoulder seam; pick up 26 sts down left neck edge; ([p4, k4] twice), p4 from front neck holder; pick up 26 sts up right neck edge; pick up 1 st between right shoulder seam and back neck holder; (114 sts on needle). Join, place marker and work in the rnd as follows:

Rnd 1: K1tbl; *p4, sl 2 sts to cn and hold at back, k2, k2 from cn**; rep from * to ** 3 times, p4; ([k1tbl, p1] 14 times), k1tbl; rep from * to ** twice, p4; (k1tbl, p1] 14 times).

Rnds 2, 3 & 4: K1tbl; *p4, k4**; rep from * to ** 3 times, p4; ([k1tbl, p1] 14 times), k1tbl; rep from * to ** twice, p4; (k1tbl, p1] 14 times).

Rep Rnds 1-4 until neck measures 1½". BO in pattern.

FINISHING
Sew sleeves to armholes. Sew side and sleeve seams. Weave in ends. Block gently to finished measurements.

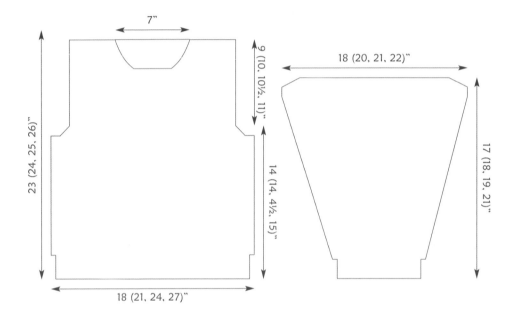

7"

9 (10, 10½, 11)"

23 (24, 25, 26)"

14 (14, 4½, 15)"

18 (21, 24, 27)"

18 (20, 21, 22)"

17 (18, 19, 21)"

annalisa cape

gregory courtney

MATERIALS

YARN: Simply Shetland Lambswool & Cashmere - 500 grams of Color A; 150 grams of Color B; 250 grams of Color C; and 150 grams of Color D. Shown in Color A, Rembrandt (994); Color B, Sienna (156); Color C, Olive Grove (1057); and Color D, Petunia (344).
NEEDLES: 60" circular US 6 (4 mm) *or correct needle to obtain gauge.* Set of 2 double-pointed US 6 (4 mm).

MEASUREMENTS
WIDTH: 41".
LENGTH: 27".

GAUGE
On US 6 in **Pattern Stitch**: 25 sts and 48 rows = 4".

DESIGNER NOTES
Knit the ruana from side to side in one piece (see schematic). Carry Color A along edge throughout. Break off and join Colors B, C and D as needed.

PATTERN STITCH (MULTIPLE OF 8 STS + 3 STS)
Row 1 (RS): With Color B, k3; *sl 1 wyib, k3; rep from *.
Row 2: With Color B, k3; *sl 1 wyif, k3; rep from *.
Row 3: With Color A, k2; *sl 1 wyib, k5, sl 1 wyib, k1; rep from *; end k1.
Row 4: With Color A, k2; *sl 1 wyif, k5, sl 1 wyif, k1; rep from *; end k1.
Row 5: With Color B, k5; *sl 1 wyib, k7; rep from * to last 6 sts; end sl 1 wyib, k5.
Row 6: With Color B, k5; *sl 1 wyif, k7; rep from * to last 6 sts; end sl 1 wyif, k5.
Rows 7-8: Rep Rows 3-4.
Rows 9-10: Rep Rows 1-2.
Rows 11-12: With Color A, knit.

RUANA
With 60" US 6 and Color A, CO 339 sts and knit 1 row.

Stripe 1: Work the 12 rows of **Pattern Stitch**.
Stripe 2: Work the 12 rows of **Pattern Stitch**, substituting Color B with Color C.
Stripe 3: Work the 12 rows of **Pattern Stitch**, substituting Color C with Color D.

Stripe 4: Work the 12 rows of **Stitch Pattern**, substituting Color D with Color C.

Continue stripe sequence as shown on schematic. On Stripe 16 (Color C), work through Row 11. On next row (Row 12), BO 168 sts, k171. Work Stripes 17-24. On Stripe 25 (Color B), work through Row 11. Turn, CO 168 sts (339 sts on needle). Work Row 12. Work Stripes 26-40. Work Stripe 41, binding off on Row 12.

ATTACHED CORDED EDGING
Begin this edging at right-most corner of lower back edge, working along right "sleeve" edge, across lower front edge, around neckline, across lower left edge, along left "sleeve" edge, and across lower back edge to where you began. On the sample, we picked up 3 out of 4 sts along horizontal edges and 1 st in every other ridge along vertical edges. You might have to pick up more or fewer sts, depending on your individual tension; be sure edges don't pull or pucker.

With double-pointed US 6 and RS of ruana facing, CO 3 sts and work as follows: *k2, sl 1, pick up 1 st on ruana edge, insert left-hand needle into fronts of picked-up st and slipped st and knit them tog. Slide sts to opposite end of needle; rep from *.

FINISHING
Weave in ends. Block gently to finished measurements.

annalisa cape

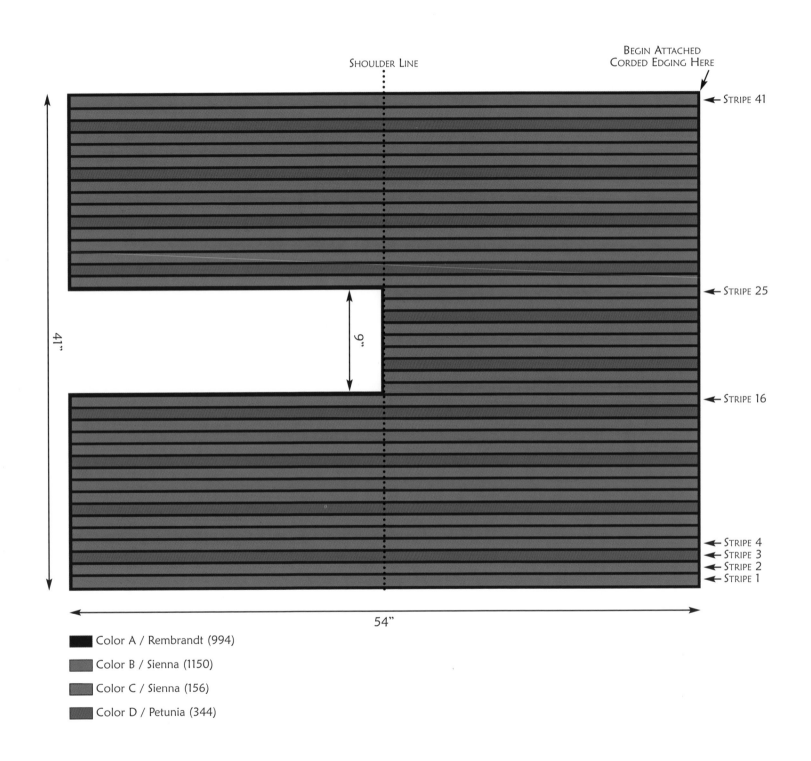

SHOULDER LINE

BEGIN ATTACHED
CORDED EDGING HERE

← STRIPE 41

← STRIPE 25

9"

← STRIPE 16

41"

← STRIPE 4
← STRIPE 3
← STRIPE 2
← STRIPE 1

54"

■ Color A / Rembrandt (994)

■ Color B / Sienna (1150)

■ Color C / Sienna (156)

■ Color D / Petunia (344)

simply **54** shetland

boatneck tee

victoria prewitt

MATERIALS

YARN: Simply Shetland Silk & Lambswool (2 strands held together throughout) - 400 (450, 500, 550) grams. Shown in Edzell (032) (2 strands held together throughout); also shown on page 60 in Venlaw (035) and Culzean (036) (1 strand of each color held together throughout).
NEEDLES: US 7 (4.5 mm),
or correct needles to obtain gauge.

MEASUREMENTS

CHEST: 36 (40, 44, 48)".
LENGTH TO UNDERARM: 15".
ARMHOLE DEPTH: 9 (9½, 10, 10½)".
LENGTH: 24 (24½, 25, 25½)".
SLEEVE LENGTH: 15 (16, 17, 18)".

GAUGE

On US 7 in st st: 16 sts and 27 rows = 4"

BACK

CO 80 (92, 100, 110) sts.

Rows 1-3: Knit.
Row 4 (RS): Purl.
Row 5: Knit.
Row 6: Purl.
Row 7: K1, sl 1, k1, psso; knit to last 3 sts; k2tog, k1.
Row 8: Purl.

Rep Rows 7-8 until 72 (80, 88, 96) sts rem, then continue in reverse st st until piece measures 15" from CO edge, ending with WS facing for next row.

SHAPE UNDERARM

BO 4 sts at beg of next 2 rows, then dec as follows:

Next Row (WS): K1, sl 1, k1, psso; knit to last 3 sts; k2tog, k1.
Next Row (RS): Purl.

Rep these last 2 rows once more. Continue in reverse st st on rem 60 (68 (76, 84) sts until armhole measures 9 (9½, 10, 10½)", ending with RS facing for next row. Work 2 rows in garter st. BO loosely.

FRONT

Work same as for back.

JOIN SHOULDERS

Place front and back tog with RS's facing each other and sew outer edges of neckline to make shoulder seams (tailor for wearer).

SLEEVES

With RS facing, pick up 72 (76, 80, 84) sts evenly around armhole (omitting bound-off sts at underarm). Work in reverse st st for 1 (1, 1, 1)" without shaping. Continue in reverse st st, **AND AT SAME TIME**, dec 1 st at beg and end of every 6th row 7 (8, 10, 10) times, then every 4th row 9 (10, 8, 10) times. Continue in reverse st st without further shaping on rem 40 (40, 44, 44) sts until sleeve measures 15 (16, 17, 18)", ending with RS facing for next row. Work 2 rows in garter st. BO loosely.

FINISHING

Sew side seams. Sew sleeve seam, including underarm bind-off. Weave in ends. Block gently to finished measurements.

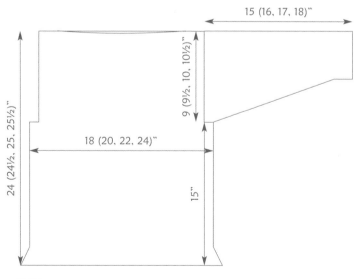

golden meadow vest

diane brown

MATERIALS

YARN: Jamieson's Shetland 2-Ply Spindrift - 50 grams of Eesit (105); 50 (50, 75, 75) grams of Natural White (104); 25 grams each of Cloud (764), Dog Rose (268), Flax (375), Fog (272) and Green Mist (274).
NEEDLES: Circular and/or double-pointed US 1 (2.50 mm) and US 3 (3.25 mm), *or correct needles to obtain gauge.*
ACCESSORIES: Stitch markers. Stitch holders.

MEASUREMENTS

CHEST: 24 (27, 30, 33)".
LENGTH TO UNDERARM: 9 (9½, 10, 11)".
ARMHOLE DEPTH: 7 (7, 7½, 8)".
LENGTH: 16 (16½, 17½, 19)".

GAUGE

On US 3 in **Chart**: 32 sts and 36 rows = 4".

ABOUT THE CHART

As garment is knit entirely in the rnd, read all rows from right to left and knit all sts in **Chart**.

BODY

With US 1 and Eesit, CO 176 (196, 216, 240) sts. Place marker, join and work as follows:

Every Rnd: *K2, p2; rep from *.

When piece measures 1", knit 1 rnd, inc'g 16 (20, 24, 24) sts evenly spaced around (192, 216, 240, 264) sts on needle). Change to US 3 and rep the 36 rnds of **Chart** until piece measures 9 (9½, 10, 11)" from CO edge.

SET ARMHOLE STEEKS AND MARK CENTER FRONT

Place first 6 (7, 8, 9) sts of rnd on holder; with alternate colors specified in the **Chart**, CO 5 sts (1 edge st and 4 steek sts); mark 1st st as beg of rnd; continue **Chart** as set on next 42 (47, 52, 57) sts; knit next st and mark as front center st; continue **Chart** as set over next 42 (47, 52, 57) sts; place next 11 (13, 15, 17) sts on another holder; CO 10 sts for steek and edge sts; continue **Chart** as set over next 85 (95, 105, 115) sts; place rem 5 (6, 7, 8) sts on first holder; CO 5 sts.

With colors used in next rnd of **Chart**, dec 1 st on each side of armhole steeks on next rnd then on following 2 (2, 2, 3)

rnds, then every other rnd 5 (6, 8, 9) times, **AND AT SAME TIME**, when 4 rnds have been worked after setting armhole steeks, beg v-neck shaping.

SET V-NECK

Work to front center st and place this st on a safety pin; CO 10 steek sts as described before; work to end of rnd. While dec'g at armholes as indicated above, dec 1 st on each side of center front steek on next rnd, then every other rnd 3 (4, 5, 7) times, then every 3rd rnd 10 (11, 11, 12) times. When all shaping is completed, you will have 20 (22, 24, 24) sts on each front shoulder and 69 (77, 83, 89) sts across back. Work without further shaping until armhole measures 7 (7, 7½, 8)". On next rnd, BO all steek sts at center front and armholes and place 29 (33, 35, 41) sts at center back on holder for neckband.

JOIN SHOULDERS

With Natural White, join front and back shoulders using either 3-needle bind-off or Kitchener st.

ARMBANDS

Cut armhole steeks through center (between 4th and 5th sts). With US 1 and Eesit, beg at center of underarm, knit 6 (7, 8, 9) sts from holder, pick up 105 (107, 113, 119) sts around armhole (into loop of edge st next to chart pattern st), and 5 (6, 7, 8) sts from holder (116, 120, 128, 136) sts on needle). Place marker for beg of rnd.

Next 2 Rnds: *K2, p2; rep from *.

Next Rnd: Knit, dec'g 14 (15, 17, 19) sts evenly spaced around (102 (105, 111, 117) sts on needle).

Next Rnd: Purl.

Next Rnd (Lace Edge): K1; *insert point of left-hand needle into front of st just knitted and knit this st tbl. Knit same st 2 more times, creating a 3-st chain. BO next 2 sts on left-hand needle; rep from * until all sts are bound off.

NECKBAND
With US 1 and Eesit, beg at left shoulder seam, pick up 45 (45, 50, 51) sts down left neck edge, k1 st from safety pin at center front neck, pick up 45 (45, 50, 51) sts up right neck edge; knit 29 (33, 35, 41) sts from holder for back neck (120 (124, 136, 144) sts on needle).

Next 2 Rnds: *K2, p2; rep from *.

Next Rnd: Knit, dec'g 15 (16, 22, 24) sts evenly spaced around (105 (108, 114, 120) sts on needle

Next Rnd: Purl.

Next Rnd: work **Lace Edge** same as for armholes. *If necessary to reduce fullness, BO 2 sts tog at each side of center front and at top of shoulders.*

FINISHING
Trim all steeks and cross stitch in place. Weave in ends. Block to finished measurements.

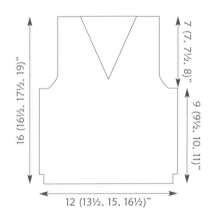

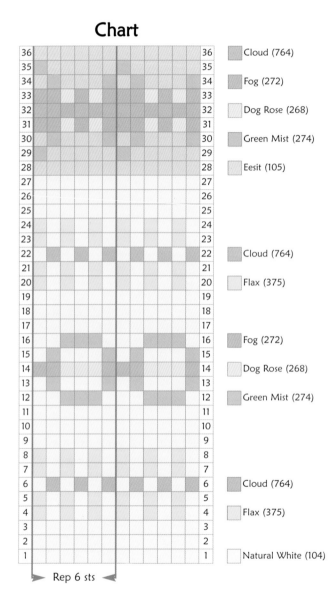

Chart

Color key:
- Cloud (764)
- Fog (272)
- Dog Rose (268)
- Green Mist (274)
- Eesit (105)
- Cloud (764)
- Flax (375)
- Fog (272)
- Dog Rose (268)
- Green Mist (274)
- Cloud (764)
- Flax (375)
- Natural White (104)

Rep 6 sts

chevron tunic

diane brown

MATERIALS

YARN: Jamieson's Shetland 2-Ply Spindrift - 275 (300, 350, 400) grams of Eesit (105); 25 grams each of Cloud (764), Flax (375), Fog (272), Green Mist (274) and Natural White (104).
NEEDLES: US 2 (3 mm) and US 3 (3.25 mm), *or correct needles to obtain gauge*. 16" circular US 2 (3 mm).
ACCESSORIES: Stitch holders. Stitch markers.

MEASUREMENTS

CHEST: 37 (40, 43½, 47)".
LENGTH TO UNDERARM: 15½ (16, 16½, 17)".
ARMHOLE DEPTH: 8 (8½, 9, 9½)".
LENGTH: 23½ (24½, 25½, 26½)".
SLEEVE LENGTH: 21 (22, 22½, 23)".

GAUGE

On US 3 in st st: 28 sts and 36 rows = 4".

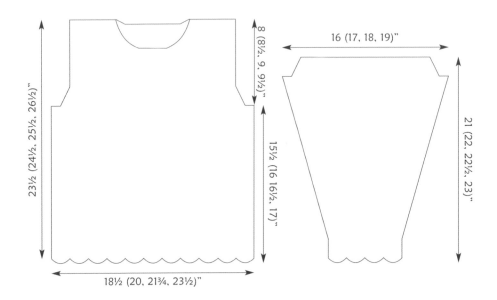

NOTES

Where only one number is given, it applies to all sizes.

ABOUT CHARTS

Read odd-numbered (RS) rows from right to left and even-numbered (WS) rows from left to right.

BACK

With US 2 and Eesit, CO 132 (145, 158, 171) sts. Work the 30 rows of **Chart A** once. Change to US 3 and work in st st, dec'g 3 (4, 5, 6) sts evenly on first row (129 (141, 153, 165) sts on needle). Continue in st st until piece measures 15½ (16, 16½, 17)" from CO edge, ending with RS facing for next row.

SHAPE ARMHOLES

BO 5 (5, 6, 6) sts at beg of next 2 rows.

Next Row (RS) (Dec Row): K2, ssk, knit to last 4 sts, k2tog, k2.
Next Row: Purl.

Rep these 2 rows 9 (9, 10, 11) more times. Work without further shaping on rem 99 (111, 119, 129) sts until armhole measures 7½ (8, 8½, 9)", ending with RS facing for next row.

SHAPE BACK NECK

Next Row (RS): K32 (36, 40, 44); BO next 35 (39, 39, 41) sts for back neck; k32 (36, 40, 44).

Turn, and working each side separately, BO at neck edge 2 sts once and 1 st 1 (1, 1, 2) times. Place rem 29 (33, 37, 40) shoulder sts on holder.

FRONT

Work same as for back until armhole measures 5 (5½, 6, 6½)", ending with RS facing for next row.

SHAPE FRONT NECK

Next Row (RS): K40 (46, 49, 53), BO next 19 (19, 21, 23) sts for front neck; k40 (46, 49, 53).

Working each side separately, BO at neck edge 3 sts once and 2 sts once, then dec 1 st on every RS row 6 (8, 7, 8) times, working opposing dec's 2 sts from neck edge as in underarm shaping. Work without further shaping on rem 29 (33, 37, 40) sts until piece measure same as back. Place shoulder sts on holders.

JOIN SHOULDERS

Join shoulders using 3-needle bind-off method.

SLEEVES

With US 2 and Eesit, CO 54 (54, 58, 58) sts. Beg and ending at points marked for your size, work the 30 rows of **Chart A** once. Change to US 3 and work in st st, inc'g 8 (8, 8, 10) sts evenly on first row (62 (62, 66, 68) sts on needle). Continue in st st, **AND AT SAME TIME**, inc 1 st at beg and end of every 4th row 14 (18, 18, 20) times, then every 6th row 11 (12, 12, 12) times (112 (120, 126, 132) sts on needle). Work without further shaping until sleeve measures 18½ (19½, 20, 20½)" from CO edge, ending with RS facing for next row.

SHAPE SLEEVE CAP

BO 5 (5, 6, 6) sts at beg of next 2 rows.

Next Row (RS) (Dec Row): K2, ssk, knit to last 4 sts, k2tog, k2.
Next Row: Purl.

Rep these 2 rows 9 (9, 10, 11) more times. BO rem 82 (90, 92, 96) sts on last WS row.

NECKBAND

With 16" US 2 and Eesit, RS facing, beg at right shoulder seam, pick up 47 (49, 49, 53)st along back neck to left shoulder seam, 31 (30, 30, 33) sts down left neck edge, 21 (21, 21, 24) sts along front neck edge, and 31 (30, 30, 33) sts up left neck edge (130 (130, 130, 143) sts on needle). Place marker to indicate beg of rnd and work the 17 rnds of **Chart B** once. BO loosely.

FINISHING

Sew sleeves into armholes. Sew side and sleeve seams. Weave in ends. Block gently to finished measurements.

Chart A
Chart B

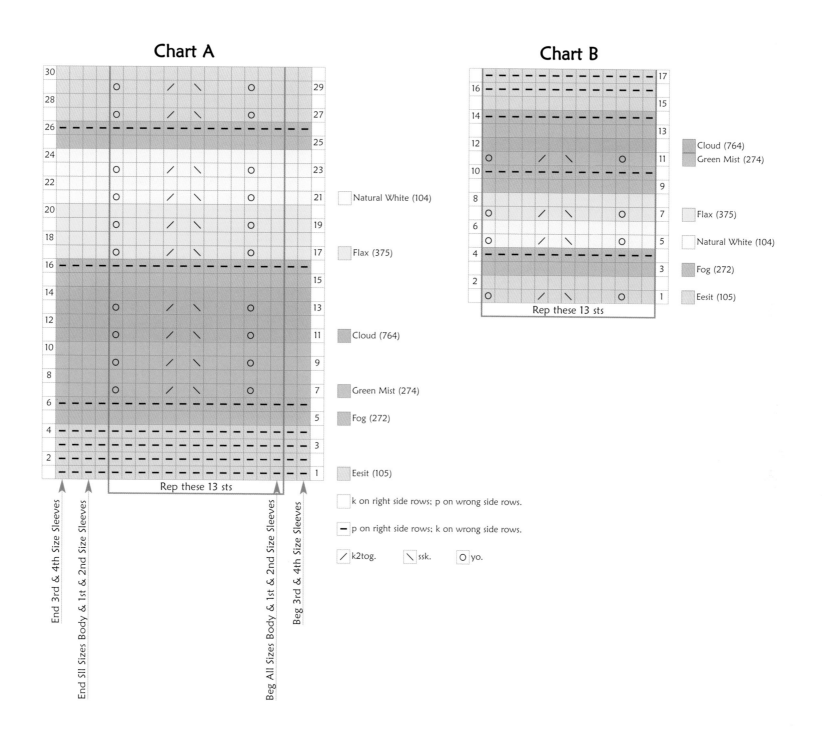

Cloud (764)
Green Mist (274)

Flax (375)

Natural White (104)

Fog (272)

Eesit (105)

Natural White (104)

Flax (375)

Cloud (764)

Green Mist (274)

Fog (272)

Eesit (105)

Rep these 13 sts

End 3rd & 4th Size Sleeves
End SII Sizes Body & 1st & 2nd Size Sleeves
Beg All Sizes Body & 1st & 2nd Size Sleeves
Beg 3rd & 4th Size Sleeves

☐ k on right side rows; p on wrong side rows.

— p on right side rows; k on wrong side rows.

╱ k2tog.   ╲ ssk.   ○ yo.

roxana jacket

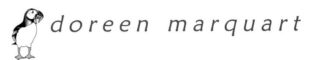

doreen marquart

MATERIALS

YARN: Simply Shetland Silk & Lambswool - 550 (650, 700, 800, 900, 1,000) grams. Hold 2 strands together throughout.
Shown in Carrick (021).
NEEDLES: US 7 (4.5 mm), *or correct needle to obtain gauge.* 16" or longer circular US 7 for collar.
Spare needle (US 7 or smaller).
Accessories: Five 1¼" buttons. Stitch markers. Stich holders.

MEASUREMENTS

CHEST: 32 (35, 38½, 41½, 45, 48)".
LENGTH TO ARMHOLE: 17 (17, 17, 18, 18, 18)".   ARMHOLE DEPTH: 9 (9, 9, 10, 10, 10)".
LENGTH: 26 (26, 26, 28, 28, 28)".   SLEEVE LENGTH: 19 (19, 19, 20, 20, 20)".

GAUGE

On US 7 in st st, holding 2 strands together throughout: 20 sts and 26 rows = 4".

LEFT BACK FLAP

CO 50 (54, 58, 62, 66, 70) sts. Work 6 rows in garter st for bottom border.

Next Row (RS): Knit.
Next Row: P40 (44, 48, 52, 56, 60), k10.

Rep these 2 rows, **AND AT SAME TIME**, dec 1 st at **end** of RS row when piece measures 3", 6" and 9". Work without further shaping on rem 47 (51, 55, 59, 63, 67) sts until piece measures 10" from CO edge, ending with RS facing for next row. Cut yarn; place stitches on spare needle to be joined later to right back flap.

RIGHT BACK FLAP

CO 50 (54, 58, 62, 66, 70) sts. Work 6 rows in garter st for bottom border.

Next Row (RS): Knit.
Next Row: K10, p40 (44, 48, 52, 56, 60).

Rep these 2 rows, **AND AT SAME TIME**, dec 1 st at **beg** of RS row when piece measures 3", 6" and 9". Work without further shaping on rem 47 (51, 55, 59, 63, 67) sts until piece measures 10" from CO edge, ending with RS facing for next row. Leave sts on needle.

JOIN FLAPS

Next Row (RS): K37 (41, 45, 49, 53, 57) sts of right back flap; with RS facing, place needle holding left back flap sts behind needle holding right back flap sts; knit next 10 sts from each needle tog; knit to end of row. *Flaps are now joined and there are 84 (92, 100, 108, 116, 124) sts on one needle.*

Continue in st st as set, always working 10 center sts in garter st, **AND AT SAME TIME**, dec 1 st at beg and end of RS row when piece measures 12" and 15". Work without further shaping on rem 80 (88, 96, 104, 112, 120) sts until piece measures 17 (17, 17, 18, 18, 18)", ending with RS facing for next row.

SHAPE ARMHOLES

Next Row (RS): K8 (8, 10, 12, 12, 12) sts and place onto a stitch holder; knit to last 8 (8, 10, 12, 12, 12) sts and place these onto another stitch holder.

Continue as set on rem 64 (72, 76, 80, 88, 96) sts until armhole measures 9 (9, 9, 10, 10, 10)" ending with RS facing for next row. Place first 20 (24, 25, 26, 30, 33) sts onto a holder for right shoulder; 24 (24, 26, 28, 28, 30) sts onto another holder for back neck; and rem 20 (24, 25, 26, 30, 33) sts onto a third holder for left shoulder.

LEFT FRONT

CO 50 (54, 58, 62, 66, 70) sts. Work 6 rows in garter st for bottom border.

Next Row (RS): Knit.
Next Row: K10, p40 (44, 48, 52, 56, 60).

Rep these 2 rows, **AND AT SAME TIME**, dec 1 st at **beg** of RS row when piece measures 3", 6", 9", 12" and 15". Work without further shaping on rem 45 (49, 53, 57, 61, 65) sts until piece measures 17 (17, 17, 18, 18, 18)", ending with RS facing for next row.

SHAPE ARMHOLE

Next Row (RS): K8 (8, 10, 12, 12, 12) sts and place onto holder; knit to end of row. Continue as set on rem 37 (41, 43, 45, 49, 53) sts until armhole measures 6 (6, 7, 7, 7, 7)", ending with WS facing for next row.

SHAPE NECK

Next Row (WS): BO 17 (17, 18, 19, 19, 20) sts; work rem 20 (24, 25, 26, 30, 33) sts.

Continue as set without further shaping until piece measures same as back. Place shoulder sts on holder.

MARK FOR BUTTONHOLES

Place markers on left front border to use as guide for buttonhole placement on right front. Place marker between 2nd and 3rd ridge from the top for top buttonhole. Place markers for 2 more buttonholes below with 12 ridges between each.

RIGHT FRONT

CO 50 (54, 58, 62, 66, 70) sts. Work 6 rows in garter st for bottom border.

Next Row (RS): Knit.
Next Row: P40 (44, 48, 52, 56, 60), k10.

Rep these 2 rows, **AND AT SAME TIME**, dec 1 st at **end** of RS row when piece measures 3", 6", 9", 12" and 15", **AND ALSO AT SAME TIME**, work **Buttonhole Rows** at the 3 points marked on left front as follows:

BUTTONHOLE ROWS—WORKED AT POINTS MARKED

Row 1 (RS): K4, BO 3, k3, knit to end of row.
Row 2: Purl to last 10 sts, k3, CO 3, k4.

After last dec at 15", continue without further shaping on rem 45 (49, 53, 57, 61, 65) sts until piece measures 17 (17, 17, 18, 18, 18)", ending with WS facing for next row.

SHAPE ARMHOLE

Next Row (WS): P8 (8, 10, 12, 12, 12) sts and place onto holder, work to end of row.
Continue as set until armhole measures 6 (6, 7, 7, 7, 7)" ending with RS facing for next row. *Remember to work your buttonholes where marked.*

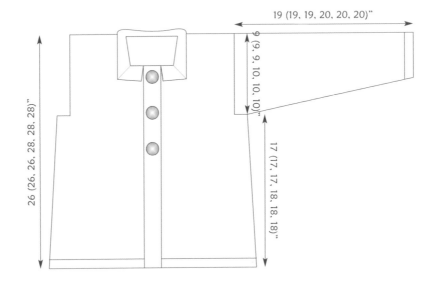

Shape Neck
Row 1 (RS): BO 17 (17, 18, 19, 19, 20) sts, work rem 20 (24, 25, 26, 30, 33) sts.

Continue as set without further shaping until piece measures same as back. Place shoulder sts on holder.

Join Shoulders
Join shoulders using 3-needle bind-off method.

Sleeves
With RS of armhole facing, knit 8 (8, 10, 12, 12, 12) sts from holder to needle; pick up 92 (92, 92, 102, 102, 102) sts evenly around armhole opening; knit the 8 (8, 10, 12, 12, 12) sts from rem holder (108 (108, 112, 126, 126, 126) sts on needle).

Next Row (WS): Purl.

Shape Underarm
Row 1 (RS): K6 (6, 8, 10, 10, 10); k2tog; knit to last 8 (8, 10, 12, 12, 12) sts; ssk; knit to end of row.
Row 2 and all WS Rows: Purl.
Row 3: K5 (5, 7, 9, 9, 9); k2tog; knit to last 7 (7, 9, 11, 11, 11) sts; ssk; knit to end of row.
Row 5: K4 (4, 6, 8, 8, 8); k2tog; knit to last 6 (6, 8, 10, 10, 10) sts; ssk; knit to end of row.

Continue in st st, dec'g as established above, until 92 (92, 92, 102, 102, 102) sts rem—*all sts previously on holders will be decreased*—ending with RS facing for next row.

Body of Sleeve
Next Row (RS) (Dec Row): K1, k2tog; knit to last 3 sts; ssk, k1.

Continue in st st as set, working **Dec Row** every 4th until there are 70 (72, 72, 78, 80, 80) on needle, then every 6th row until there are 50 (52, 54, 58, 58, 60) sts on needle. Continue without further shaping until sleeve measures 18 (18, 18, 19, 19, 19)", ending with RS facing for next row. Work in garter st for 7 rows, binding off on last WS row.

Collar
With WS facing, omitting buttonband, pick up 23 (23, 25, 27, 27, 29) up left neck edge; knit 24 (24, 26, 28, 28, 30) sts from back stitch holder; pick up 23 (23, 25, 27, 27, 29) down left neck edge, omitting buttonhole band (70 (70, 76, 82, 82, 88) sts on needle).

Next Row (RS): K7 (7, 8, 9, 9, 10); place marker; k16 (16, 17, 18, 18, 19); place marker; k24 (24, 26, 28, 28, 30); place marker; k16 (16, 17, 18, 18, 19); place marker; k7 (7, 8, 9, 9, 10).

Work 15 (17, 19, 21, 23, 25) rows in garter stitch, **AND AT SAME TIME**, inc 1 st before and after each marker—*knit into front then back of st*—every other row. BO on last RS row.

Finishing
Sew underarm and side seams. Sew on buttons opposite buttonholes. Sew two buttons on back flap, the first where flaps join and the other halfway between first button and bottom of jacket. Weave in ends. Block to finished measurements.

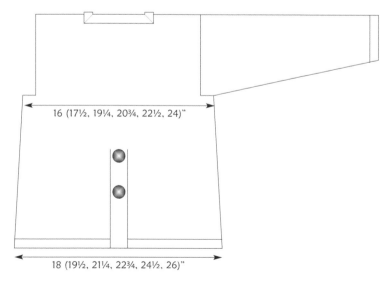

16 (17½, 19¼, 20¾, 22½, 24)"

18 (19½, 21¼, 22¾, 24½, 26)"

whirligig vest

betsy westman

MATERIALS

YARN: Colorway 1 (Pages 86-87) - Jamieson's Shetland 2-Ply Spindrift - 50 grams of Color A, Crimson (525); 25 grams each of Color B, Ginger (462); Color C, Maroon (595); Color D, Mint (770); Color E, Loganberry (1290); Color F, Admiral Navy (727); Color G, Chartreuse (365); Color H, Daffodil (390); Color I, Teviot (136); Color J, Lilac (620); and Color K, Leprechaun (259).

Colorway 2 (Opposite Page) - 50 grams of Color A, Shaela (102); 25 grams each of Color B, Shetland Black (101); Color C, Mogit (107); Color D, Black/Sholmit (110); Color E, Mooskit/Shaela (115); Color F, Eesit (105); Color G, Sholmit (103); Color H, Moorit/Eesit (116); Color I, Natural White (104); Color J, Shaela/White (112); and Color K, Moorit (108).

Colorway 3 (Page 84) - 50 grams of Color A, Sunrise (187); 25 grams each of Color B, Cornfield (410); Color C, Ginger (462); Color D, Peat (198); Color E, Madder (587); Color F, Nutmeg (1200); Color G, Sunglow (185); Color H, Sunset (186); Color I, Flame (271); Color J, Crimson (525); and Color K, Buttercup (182).

NEEDLES: 16" & 32" circular US 2 (3 mm), *or correct needles to obtain gauge*.

ACCESSORIES: Stitch markers. Stitch holders.

MEASUREMENTS

CHEST: 36 (38½, 40½, 42½, 45)".
LENGTH TO UNDERARM: 11 (11, 12, 13, 13)".
ARMHOLE DEPTH: 10 (10, 10½, 10½, 11)".
LENGTH: 21 (21 22½, 23½, 24)".

GAUGE

On US 3 in **Chart**: 30 sts and 29 rows = 4".

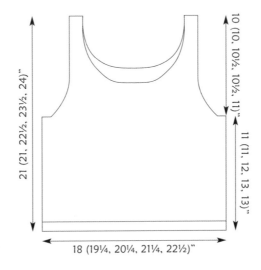

21 (21, 22½, 23½, 24)"

10 (10, 10½, 10½, 11)"

11 (11, 12, 13, 13)"

18 (19¼, 20¼, 21¼, 22½)"

DESIGNER NOTES
Knit body in the round up to armhole, then work in rows to shoulders. You won't work all the rows in the **Chart**; work until the length specified for your size.

BODY
With Color A and 32" circular US 2, CO 272 (288, 304, 320, 336) sts. Place marker at beg of rnd, join and work in the rnd as follows:

Next 6 Rows: *K1, p1; rep from *.

Work **Chart** until piece measures 11 (11, 12, 13, 13)" from CO edge.

DIVIDE FOR FRONT AND BACK
Next Rnd: BO 8 sts; work 120 (128, 136, 144, 152) sts in pattern as set; BO 16 sts; work 120 (128, 136, 144, 152) sts in pattern as set and place on holder for back; BO rem 8 sts of rnd. Break yarn.

SHAPE FRONT ARMHOLES AND FRONT NECK
Turn, rejoin yarn, and working back and forth in rows on front of body only, continue in pattern as set, **AND AT SAME TIME**, dec 1 st at beg and end of every row 8 (8, 9, 9, 10) times, every other row 9 (9, 10, 10, 11) times, and every 4th row 7 (7, 9, 9, 11) times. **ALSO AT SAME TIME**, when armhole measures 3 (3, 3½, 3½, 4)", *while continuing to shape armholes*, BO center 16 sts on next RS row, and working each side separately, BO 3 sts at neck edge once, then dec 1 st at neck edge on next 6 (7, 7, 7, 7) rows, then every other row 8 (10, 10, 10, 10) times, and every 4th row 3 (4, 4, 4, 4) times. Work without further shaping on rem 8 (8, 8, 12, 12) sts until armhole measures 10 (10, 10½, 10½, 11)". BO.

SHAPE BACK ARMHOLES AND BACK NECK
Move back sts from holder onto needle, rejoin yarn and working back and forth in rows, shape armholes same as for front. **ALSO AT SAME TIME**, when armhole measures 5 (5, 5½, 5½, 6)", *while continuing to shape armholes*, BO center 20 sts on next RS row, and working each side separately, BO 4 sts at neck edge once, then dec 1 st at neck edge on next 6 (7, 7, 7, 7) rows, then every other row 8 (10, 10, 10, 10) times, and every 4th row 0 (1, 1, 1, 1) times. Work without further shaping on rem 8 (8, 8, 12, 12) sts until armhole measures same as front. BO.

ARMBANDS
With 16" US 3 and Color A, RS facing, pick up 164 (164, 172, 172, 180) sts evenly around armhole edges, place marker, join and work in the rnd as follows:

Next 6 Rnds: *K1, p1; rep from *.

BO.

NECKBAND
With 16" US 3 and Color A, RS facing, pick up 216 evenly around neck edge, place marker, join and work in the rnd as follows:

Next 6 Rnds: *K1, p1; rep from *.

BO.

FINISHING
Sew shoulder seams. Block to finished measurements.

Chart

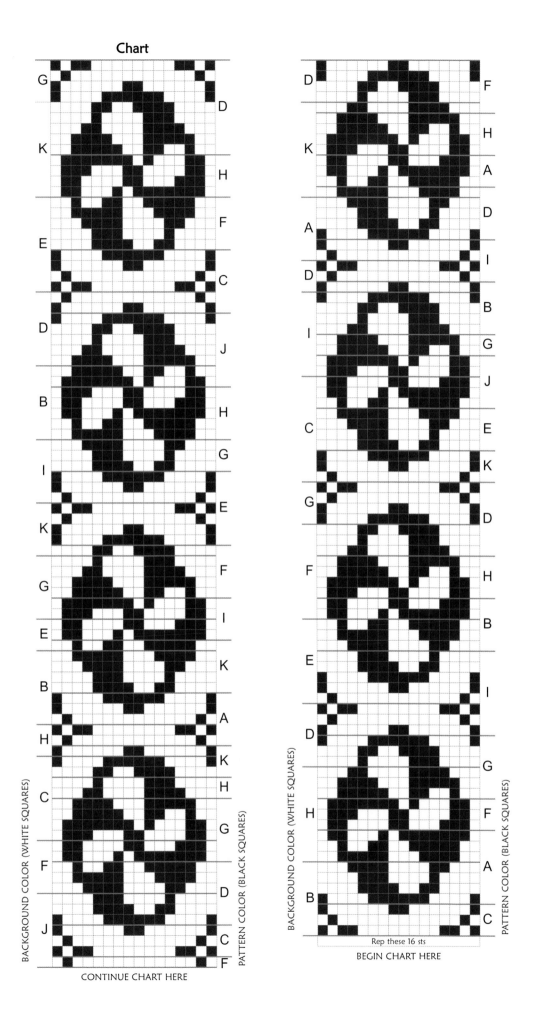

BACKGROUND COLOR (WHITE SQUARES)

PATTERN COLOR (BLACK SQUARES)

CONTINUE CHART HERE

Rep these 16 sts

BEGIN CHART HERE

ziggy cap

chris rieffer

MATERIALS

YARN: Simply Shetland Lambswool & Cashmere - 100 grams. Shown in Red Hot (1294).
NEEDLES: US 4 (3.5 mm),
or correct needles to obtain gauge.

MEASUREMENTS

CIRCUMFERENCE: 20".
LENGTH: 8".

GAUGE

On US 4 in **Chart**: 28 sts and 36 rows = 4".

DESIGNER NOTE

Knit this cap in a medium to dark color; it will show off the cables to their best advantage.

CAP

CO 140 sts. Work Rows 1-12 of **Chart** 4 times, then work Rows 13-38 once.

FINISHING

Cut yarn, leaving a 6" tail, thread onto darning needle and draw through rem 7 sts. Pull tight, push to inside of cap and weave in ends. Block gently.

Key

 k.

— p.

sl 1 st to cn and hold at front; k1; k1 from cn.

sl 1 st to cn and hold at back; k2; p1 from cn.

sl 2 sts to cn and hold at front; p1; k2 from cn.

╲ ssk.

╱ k2tog.

⚠2 p2tog.

⚠3 p3tog.

■ no stitch.

Chart

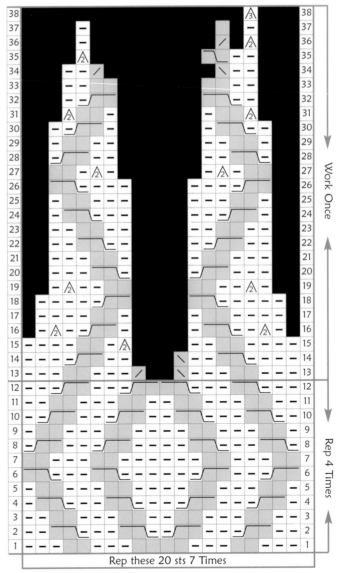

Rep these 20 sts 7 Times